joke
-a-
thon

Silver Dolphin

Silver Dolphin Books
An imprint of Printers Row Publishing Group
10350 Barnes Canyon Road, Suite 100, San Diego, CA 92121
www.silverdolphinbooks.com

Copyright © 2016 make believe ideas ltd

All notations of errors or omissions should be addressed to Silver Dolphin Books, Editorial Department, at the above address. All other correspondence (author inquiries, permissions) concerning the content of this book should be addressed to:
make believe ideas ltd

The Wilderness, Berkhamsted, Hertfordshire, HP4 2AZ, UK.
501 Nelson Place, P.O. Box 141000, Nashville, TN 37214-1000, USA.
www.makebelieveideas.com

ISBN: 978-1-68412-024-6

Manufactured, printed, and assembled in China.

20 19 18 17 16 1 2 3 4 5

ARE YOU READY FOR A JOKE-A-THON?

This book is bursting with every kind of joke you can imagine!

Jam-packed with the best knock-knock jokes, doctor-doctor ticklers, animal gags, and funny messages around, this book contains everything you need to keep your audience laughing!

There is even space at the back of the book for you to record any other side-splitters you hear along the way, as well as room to make up your own!

Prepare to never be bored again!

WARNING: This book is not suitable for people who lack a sense of humor!

Why did the snake go to school?

To study hissstory!

Why are noses always putting their hands up?

Because they love to be picked!

Why did the toilet go to the doctor?

Because it felt a little FLUSHED!

Why did the brainiac eat her homework?

Because she thought it was a piece of cake!

Why did the man cut a hole in his umbrella?

So he could see when it stopped raining!

Why did the broom get married so fast?

Because she was swept off her feet!

Why didn't the snowman go to the disco?

Because he had tickets to the snow ball!

Why did the tomato blush?

Because he saw the salad dressing!

Why did the man take a clock on the plane?

He wanted to see time fly!

Why did the monster eat the flashlight?

He wanted a light snack!

Why did the gelatin wobble?
Because he saw the milk shake!

Why did the elevator visit the doctor?
Because it came down with a cold!

Why did the music-loving boy stick a shoe to his ear?
Because he liked SOUL music!

Why did the man sit on a clock?
He was told to work overtime!

Why did the man hang his cell phone from the ceiling?
Because he was told it was a mobile phone!

Why did the vegetable house need a new roof?

Because it was full of leeks!

Why did the cookie go to the hospital?

Because it felt crummy!

Why did the lightbulb fail its exams?

It wasn't very bright!

Why did the moon burp?

Because it was full!

Why did the teacher wear dark glasses?

Because her students were too bright!

Why did the computer feel sick?

It had too many chips!

Why did the fungus want a bigger house?

He didn't have mushroom!

Why did the computer hide his cheese?

So the mouse wouldn't eat it!

Why did the bean run away from the farm?

The farmer was picking on him!

Why did the apartment building become a library?

Because it had so many stories!

What did the kettle say when the pot lost his temper?

Just SIMMER down!

What did the dice say when the cards refused to shuffle?

I'll DEAL with you later!

How do you stop your phone battery from running out?

Hide its sneakers!

What did the ocean say to the lifeguard?
Nothing, it just waved!

Have you seen the new onion website?

Yes, it's a SITE for sore eyes!

Which vampire lives in a kitchen drawer?

Count SPATULA!

Why are noses with colds so fit?

Because they're always running!

YAWN!

Why was the meatball tired?

Because it was pasta its bedtime!

What kind of vegetables do you find in the gym?

Muscle sprouts!

What goes HA! HA! BONK!

A man laughing his head off!

OOPS!

What has teeth but cannot eat?

A zipper!

How do you make a toilet roll?

Push it down a hill!

What did the sun say to the cloud when he went on vacation?

You'll be MIST!

What do you get if you put your pen in the freezer?

Iced ink?

Well, yes, you do stink, but that's not the answer!

Where's the best place to make noise online?

The DIN-ternet!

CRASH

Why was the shirt sad?

Because the jeans were blue!

When should you never suck your food?

Chewsday!

sniff! Why was the skeleton feeling lonely?

Because he had NO BODY to play with!

What do elves do after school?

Their gnomework!

How do fishermen catch virtual fish?

Online!

Why are scarfs bad at sports?

Because they prefer to hang around!

When's the best time to chop down a tree?

Sep-timber!

Which famous sea creature never tidies its room?

The Loch Mess Monster!

What did Mr. Volcano say to Mrs. Volcano when they got married?

I lava you!

Which sweet treat makes lots of mistakes?

D'oh-nuts!

What did the curtains
say to the window?

We've got you covered!

How does the ocean wear its hair?

Wavy!

What sound did the grape
make when it got squashed?

A little wine!

What type of ice cream
does Frankenstein eat?

Cookies 'n' scream!

What do sea monsters eat at parties?

Ships 'n' dip!

Why didn't the artist
leave his bedroom?

**Because he liked
drawing curtains!**

Where do astronauts keep their sandwiches?

In a launch box!

What lives at the bottom
of the ocean and shakes?

A nervous wreck!

What's green and refuses
to join in games?

The incredible sulk!

Did you hear about the plumber who couldn't fix the pipes?

His business went down the drain!

Did you hear about the angry man who mistook his soap for cheese?

He was foaming at the mouth!

Where does the President of the United States keep his armies?

Up his sleevies!

Why do pirates keep soap under their hats?

To help them wash ashore!

Where is Timbuktu?

Next to Timbukone!

Timbuktu

Timbukone

What did the books say when they couldn't agree?

We're just not on the same page!

What do you get if you have two running faucets?

A race!

What goes up and down but never moves?

A flight of stairs!

Which worms have spines?

Bookworms!

BIG BOOK OF INSECTS
BY KAT A. PILLAR

Which footwear will make you jump?

Boo-ts!

Did you hear about the shop
full of overgrown trees?

They had to hire a branch manager!

How do snowmen get to work?

On bICICLES!

Why do monsters eat metal pins?

It's their staple diet!

Why couldn't the doctor see her patients?

Because she'd lost her glasses!

How do you know when it's been
raining cats and dogs?

The ground is covered in poodles!

What's a cow's favorite dance?

The moo-nwalk!

What do you call a man with
a car on his head?

Jack!

Did you hear about the woman who lived next to a wall?

**She broke her ladder
and never got over it!**

Why did the man throw away
his paper pants?

Because they were tearable!

Why are hairdressers
never late for work?

Because they know all the shortcuts!

What did the rockstar do when he locked himself out?

He sang until he found the right key!

Which vegetables will you find on a clothes hanger?

Jacket potatoes!

How do you know if a train is eating gum?

Because you can hear it chew, chew, chew!

Why were the company directors yawning?

They were having a BORED meeting!

When is the best time to visit the dentist?

Tooth hurty!

FUNNY MESSAGES

There's going to be a storm!

Gustov Wynd

I'd recommend this book.

Paige Turner

Wait here for me!

Isa Cumming

The weather's terrible!

Reyna Lott

What's that noise?

Cara Larm

Where do polar bears keep their money?

In snowbanks!

Where does a skunk do its washing up?

In the kitchen STINK!

What do you call an alligator in a vest?

An investigator!

What do you call a fish with no eyes?

Fsh!

What did the frog order from the burger bar?

A CROAK and FLIES!

How do you stop your dog from barking in the back of your car?

Put it in the front!

Why do cows wear bells?

Because their horns don't work!

What do you call a bee in a bell tower?

A humdinger!

What do cats eat for breakfast?

Mice Krispies!

What's a shark's favorite sandwich?

Peanut butter and jellyfish!

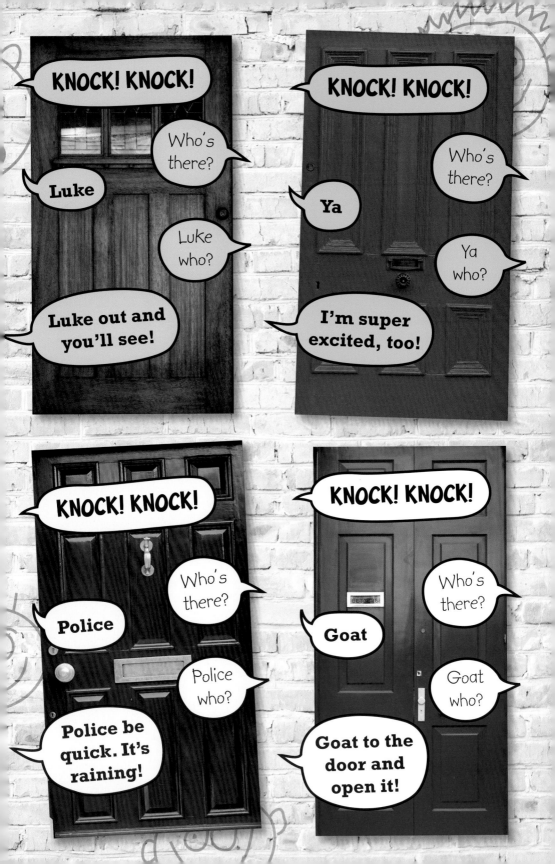

What's a fisherman's favorite musical instrument?

The cast-a-nets!

What's the best snack to eat on a rollercoaster?

F-RISE and dip!

How did the gnome get indigestion?

By goblin his food!

How did the tap dancer break his leg?

He fell in the sink!

Where do barbers keep their money?

In shaving accounts!

Why doesn't gravity have many friends?

Because it brings everyone down!

Why are mushrooms always invited to parties?

Because they are fun-guys!

What's green and sniffs?

A cucumber with a cold!

How did the cyclist puncture his tire?

He drove over a fork in the road!

What's red and hairy and goes up and down?

A raspberry in an elevator!

What lives underground and uses bad language?

Crude oil!

!*!*!*

Why do fleas never pay train fares?

They prefer itch-hiking!

itch
itch
itch
itch
flea ville

Did you hear about the scientist who broke the laws of gravity?

He got a suspended sentence!

Did you hear about the scouts' chess tournament?

It was in tents!

Did you hear about the man with size 18 boots?

Finding shoes was no small feet!

What's the longest word in the world?

Smile, because there's a mile after the S!

Waitress, will my spaghetti be long?

Yes, sir, would you like me to cut it up for you?

Did you hear about the car that couldn't turn left?

It was all right in the end!

What's a pirate's favorite letter?

Arrrr!

Did you hear about the chef who was crazy for pastries?

She was a doughnut!

How do mountains keep their ears warm?

They wear snowcaps!

What do you say when you meet
a three-headed alien?

Hello!   **Hello!**   **Hello!**

Why should you always wear
glasses for math?

Because they improve di-vision! $6 \div 2 = 3$

Why is a calculator a faithful friend?

Because you can always count on it!

What do you call an
alien with no name?

Nothing!

What did cavemen use to cut down trees?

Dino-SAWS!

Which snack tastes best on a ghost train?

I scream!

Why was the computer full of holes?

Someone had taken bytes out of it!

What has four legs but can't walk?

A table!

What do you call a cheese that's not yours?

Nacho cheese!

Why couldn't the teddy bear eat any cake?

Because it was stuffed!

Which letters are not in the alphabet?

The ones in the mail!

What did the soccer ball say
to the goalkeeper?

I get a kick out of you!

What should you say when
you meet a steep rock face?

Hi, Cliff!

What do you call a man with leaves in his boots?

Russell!

What do you call fake pasta?

Mockeroni!

What did the cola do after knitting a scarf?

Soda dress!

What do you call a fairy who has fallen in manure?

Stinkerbell!

Why can't you order a clown fish in a restaurant?

Because it tastes funny!

How do you make a hotdog stand?

Hide its chair!

What's orange and sounds like a parrot?

A carrot!

What do clouds wear under their jeans?

Thunderpants!

What's the best way to get a fish online?

Catch it Internet!

What do elves learn at school?

The elf-abet!

When did the pencil stop talking?

When it got to the point!

How much does it cost to pierce a pirate's ear?

A buccaneer!

Why do dentists never lie?

Because they always tell the tooth!

What's Tarzan's favorite lesson?

Hippopot-a-math!

1 + 1 =

What has a lot of heads and tails but no body?

A pocket full of change!

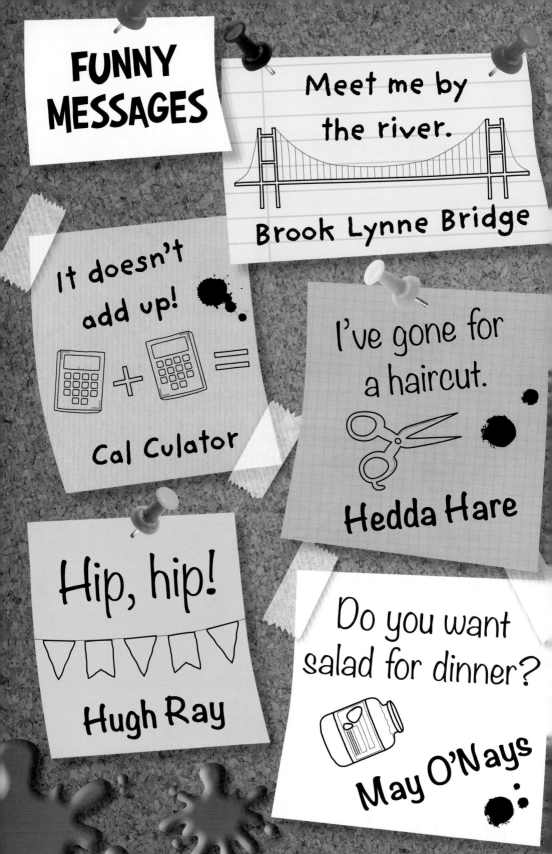

The police are after me!

Robyn Banks

What did he say?

Candy B. Hurd

Got to run or I'll miss my bus!

Nick Ovtime

Meet you on the top floor.

Ella Vader

What would you like for lunch?

Chi Spurger

If seagulls fly over the sea, what flies over the bay?

Bagels!

Why don't cats like the color green?

Because they prefer purr-ple!

What do elephants wear to the beach?

Swimming trunks!

What type of dog works in a hair salon?

A shampoodle!

Why don't grasshoppers cry?

Because they're always hoppy!

Which animal should you never play with?

A cheetah!

How do you stop dogs chasing people on bikes?

Give them skateboards!

What kind of bugs do you find in libraries?

Bookworms!

How do toads guide their boats through the mist?

With frog horns!

Where do cows go when it rains?

To the mooovies!

Why couldn't the pony sing?

Because he was a little HORSE!

Where do frogs keep their money?

In riverbanks!

What did the spider say to the fly?

I'm so pleased to eat you!

What do you call a camel with three humps?

Humphrey!

When do birds go to hospital?

When they need tweetment!

Why doesn't Tarzan need a calculator?

Because the jungle is full of adders!

Why do storks stand on one leg?

Because they'd fall over if they lifted both!

What's black and white and goes up and down?

A zebra in an elevator!

Why did the elephant miss his flight?

He spent too long packing his trunk!

Which dinosaur worked on construction sites?

Tyrannosaurus wrecks!

Doctor, Doctor, I think I'm a baby cod!

Sounds a little fishy to me!

Doctor, Doctor, I think I'm a submarine!

You're clearly out of your depth!

Doctor, Doctor, I think I'm a yo-yo!

How do you feel?

Sometimes I'm up and sometimes I'm down!

Doctor, Doctor, I've got a blocked nose!

How do you smell?

Terrible!

Doctor, Doctor, my nose is 11 inches long!

Come back if it grows into a foot!

Why did the coffee taste like mud?
Because it was fresh ground!

Why did the banana go to hospital?
Because it wasn't peeling well!

Why did the student study on a plane?
She wanted a higher education!

Why did the toilet get a gold seat?
Because it was feeling flush!

Why did the woman put blush on her forehead?

She was trying to makeup her mind!

Why did the policeman refuse to get out of bed?

He wanted to work undercover!

Why did the eyes give up teaching?

Because they only had two pupils!

1+1=?

Why did the car refuse to move?

Because its wheels were tired!

Why didn't the knife trust the spoon?

Because the spoon kept stirring things up!

Why did the woman put bowls of milk and water in her garden?

She heard it was going to rain cats and dogs!

Why did the gray pebble
wear bright purple pants?
**He wanted to be
a little bolder!**

Why did the picture go to jail?
Because it was framed!

Why didn't anyone eat the overripe banana?
Because it wasn't a-peeling!

Why did the socks sit in the fruit bowl?
They were told they were a pear!

Why did the lady have her hair in a bun?
Because she'd eaten all her burgers!

What did the carpet say
to the floorboards?

I've got you covered!

Why do golfers carry spare socks?

In case they get a hole in one!

Why are soccer players messy eaters?

Because they are always dribbling!

Why was the belt arrested?

For holding up the pants!

How many ears do cowboys have?

**Three: a left ear, a right ear,
and a wild frontier!**

Where do football players eat Thanksgiving dinner?

The supper bowl!

What's yellow and sneezes?

A lemon with a cold!

How do sports stars stay cool?

They sit next to their fans!

Why did the girl sit on the ladder to sing?

She wanted to hit the high notes!

How did the lamp feel when its bulb burned out?

De-lighted!

What did the tree say
to the boulder?

You rock!

Why is the ocean so messy?

**Because the fish never
make the seabed!**

What did the sand say when
the sea asked for a date?

Shore!

How do you make a milk shake?

Tell it a scary story!

Which part of a tree makes cats jump?

The bark!

How do you make a cheese puff?

Chase it round the supermarket!

What did the tree say when it was feeling sad?

Just leaf me alone!

What's the ocean's favorite game?

Tide and seek!

Why did the banana miss school?

It was peeling bad!

Why are trees always ready for a swim?

Because they are never without their trunks!

Why was Cinderella bad at sports?

She was always running from the ball!

Why do babies make good basketball players?

Because they are good at dribbling!

Why are Olympians bad DJs?

Because they are always breaking records!

Why was the singer locked out of her house?

She couldn't find the right key!

Who can jump higher than the Empire State Building?

Everyone—the Empire State Building can't jump!

MY JOKES

Whenever you hear a good joke, write it down here so you won't forget it.